Land

D0366436

Dona Herweck Rice

Consultant

Timothy Rasinski, Ph.D
Kent State University

Publishing Credits

Dona Herweck Rice, *Editor-in-Chief*

Lee Aucoin, *Creative Director*

Conni Medina, M.A.Ed., *Editorial Director*

Jamey Acosta, *Editor*

Robin Erickson, *Designer*

Stephanie Reid, *Photo Editor*

Rachelle Cracchiolo, M.S.Ed., *Publisher*

Based on writing from *TIME For Kids.*

Teacher Created Materials

5301 Oceanus Drive
Huntington Beach, CA 92649-1030
http://www.tcmpub.com
ISBN 978-1-4333-3574-7
© 2012 Teacher Created Materials, Inc.
Made in China
Nordica.022015.CA21401962

There are many
kinds of land.

What land do you see?

See the desert.
It is dry.

See the grassland.
It is grassy.

See the mountain.
It is tall.

See the rain forest.
It is wet.

See the beach.
It is sandy.

See the forest.
It is tall.

See the canyon.
It is deep.

Words to Know

are

beach

canyon

deep

desert

do

dry

forest

grassland

grassy

is

it

kinds

land

many

mountain

of

rain forest

sandy

see

tall

the

there

wet

what

you